Silvia Ostertag

# Finding Silence – and Living from it

Matador
9 Priory Business Park,
Wistow Road, Kibworth Beauchamp,
Leicestershire. LE8 0RX
Tel: 0116 279 2299
Email: books@troubador.co.uk
Web: www.troubador.co.uk/matador
Twitter: @matadorbooks

ISBN 978 1788036 368

British Library Cataloguing in Publication Data.
A catalogue record for this book is available from the British Library.

Printed and bound by CPI Group (UK) Ltd, Croydon, CR0 4YY
Typeset in 12pt Bembo by Troubador Publishing Ltd, Leicester, UK

Matador is an imprint of Troubador Publishing Ltd

Silvia Ostertag

# Finding Silence – and Living from it

## Hints and Prompts for Every Day

Translated from the German by
Susanne Ehrhardt and Wendy R. Tyndale

# CONTENTS

TRANSLATORS' NOTE     i

AUTHOR'S THANKS     ii

INTRODUCTION     iii

AT THE THRESHOLD OF THE DAY     1

For the first time     2
Beginner     3
Like a mountain     4
Silence     6
Letting yourself arrive     7
A mayfly     8
Centre and distance     9
All right     10
Expecting     11
In expectation     12
Readiness     13

Spectator     14
I do not know     16
Complete     17
Forcing the breath     18
Must and cannot     19
Difficult     20
Not calculating     21
Chop or skedaddle     22
Suffering     24
Old discontents     26

Processing                    28
Peace                         29

To what end?                  30
What for?                     31
Where to?                     32
Not-thinking                  33
Becoming stupid               34
Insight                       35
Recuperation                  36
Out                           37

Smiling                       38
Sleeping longer               39
Playing                       40
Carnival time                 41
Lent                          42
Birthday                      43
All Souls                     44
Non-holiday                   46
Planets                       48
Daybreak                      50

Familiar                      51
NOW and time                  52
Now                           53
No time                       54
Missing silence               55
Habit                         56
Red sky in the morning        57
As with a plant               58
Why not?                      60

## IN THE MIDST OF IT                                       61

*In the midst of it - Steps*                               62
Is it this?                                                62
This step                                                  62
Eyes and legs                                              63
Mountain, grass and cow                                    63
Walking in the mist                                        64
Golden autumn wind                                         65
Snow                                                       66
Easy                                                       66

*In the midst of it – Pausing*                             67
What is real                                               67
We cannot miss it                                          68
Responsible                                                69
Bad                                                        69
There it is again                                          70
Bad things                                                 71
Pain                                                       72
Why?                                                       73
Wonderful now                                              74
The gates of truth                                         75
Traffic light                                              75
What concerns me                                           76

*In the midst of it – Acting*                              77
Get up!                                                    77
Laughter                                                   78
Playtime                                                   79
Being present                                              80
Attending                                                  81
Being wholly present                                       82
Bridge                                                     83
Collecting stillness                                       84

Even more silent                    85
Being really silent                 86
Present                             86
Responsibility                      87
Everyday is the way                 88
Every action                        89

*In the midst of it – Pausing again*   90
Enlightenment                       90
Then                                91
I                                   92
Free time                           94
Stupid                              95
Anger                               96
Looking into                        97
Ugly stain                          98
Prompt                              99
Failing to catch the silence        100
Rain and wind                       100
May no-one be forgetful             101

AT THE THRESHOLD OF THE
NIGHT                               103

Waking to yourself                  104
Simple                              105
Earth gratitude                     106
Evening question                    107
Not yet                             108
Summer evening                      109
Now is not                          110
How can it grow silent?             111
Not a good day                      112
A good day                          113
Independence                        114

Leaving it                             115
Megalomania                            116
Attached                               117
Moulding                               118
Deceptive thoughts                     120
Tiger, goose, mouse and monkey         121
Fear                                   122
The quieter                            123
Silence makes us happy                 124
Reconciliation                         125
There you sit                          126

Play                                   127
Looking                                128
In the midst of it                     129
Winter                                 130
Winter solstice                        131
I wonder                               132
Advent                                 134
Good will                              135
Shared space                           136
Until                                  137

GUIDANCE ON PRACTICE                   139

On posture                             140
Picturing the flow of breath           142

# TRANSLATORS' NOTE

After we had translated Silvia Ostertag's first book, 'Living Silence', we started wondering about working on this, her second one and therefore welcomed the invitation from the Oxford Zen Centre to do so.

As with 'Living Silence', Silvia's creative and beautiful use of German, through which she strives to put the ineffable into words, was a challenge for us but we hope that our attempts to draw out her meaning and translate it into accessible English have borne fruit. For us, the work has again provided an opportunity to delve into the depths of Silvia's teaching and we have greatly enjoyed it.

We would like to thank all those who have encouraged us along the way, especially Albrecht and Johanna Ostertag, whose enthusiasm about the idea gave us confidence. We are also grateful to Sandy Bharat for dedicating so much time, energy and skill to the preparation of the manuscript for publication.

Susanne Ehrhardt and Wendy Tyndale
Oxford, August 2016.

# AUTHOR'S THANKS

The prompts and guidance put together in this book have all arisen from time spent with people who have practised silence with me as a form of meditation and, going on from there, as a continuous practice in everyday life. So my thanks are due to them, both for the inspiration they have given to my own practice and for their listening ear which has led me to put some of my thoughts into words.

In addition, and above all, I feel grateful every day to Karlfried Graf Dürkheim, Willigis Jäger Kyo-un Ken and also Masamichi Yamada Ryo-un Ken for having been my teachers.

I thank my husband for going through my writing with a critical eye and for his help in choosing the texts. I also thank Helga Gramlich for her valuable advice from the reader's point of view.

# INTRODUCTION

## FINDING SILENCE AND LIVING FROM IT

Who wants to find silence? And live from it? Anyone who loves silence. These texts have been written in order to deepen and broaden the love of silence. To find silence brings happiness in a way that has nothing to do with the temporary feeling of well-being which we experience when our needs are met and our wishes fulfilled. When we experience the happiness connected with silence, we do not know how to explain it or give a reason for it. We cannot even call it an emotion. It is simply a natural state of being, as though there could be nothing else.

But even those of us who have not yet experienced this effect of silence will have an inkling of what is meant because of our deep-seated natural interest. For as soon as we suffer in any way at all from today's noise, from the din outside or from the uproar within, we look for silence. Then – even though far away – silence appears as a desirable contrast to the tormenting now. But if we experience it, this silence, it is surprisingly familiar and – perhaps just for a moment – it encompasses every sound and penetrates all inner tumult. If we experience it, then the silent now is suddenly as spacious as if all time belonged to it.

So the silence which is the subject of this book can be seen as a root and at the same time as something all-embracing. It can be seen as something within ourselves which has always been familiar. It can be seen as something which wants us to hear it, as something which allows us to search for it; as though we had always known about it, as though we originated from it, as though we wanted to find it again, as though we wanted to find ourselves again within it.

We think we are lost, we feel separated from ourselves. Ever since the moment when we learnt to differentiate and, through this supreme gift, dared to become individuals, we have forgotten our being-one with the One-being[1], the ground of our soul. In order to save ourselves we fight against an imaginary enemy until, on the edge of the abyss of mutual destruction, we wake up to the question of the real meaning of this process. It is from there that we seek and find one way or another of moving beyond the stage of the differentiating, dualistic perspective, with the aim of finding ourselves again on a conscious level in our being-one with this One-being.

There we will recognise that we have never left this being-one and that the drama of separation is nothing but the blessed illusion thanks to which we are able to recognise the One-being. If such an experience takes hold of us, or even just brushes past us, we feel completely whole in the midst of all the conflict which has gone along with our development into an objectifying consciousness. The strange longing which has accompanied humankind as a sort of countermovement to every step in our development towards a more differentiating understanding, this longing is satisfied, without our ever taking a step backwards.

---

[1] Translators' note: This, as in the text 'Suffering' (page 24), refers to the notion of being, not to any existing entity. The German 'Sein' here is the verbal noun of 'sein', meaning 'to be'.

To follow the track of silence is a possible way to attain such an experience. When we experience silence, it is as if it entirely absorbed us into itself and as if it absorbed everything around us in the same way. If we commit ourselves entirely to it, it is as if we created ourselves out of it. It is as if all beings and things created themselves anew from it at every moment.

And in the afterglow of such an experience which, although it feels so utterly natural, is suddenly over, in this afterglow, it is as if silence affected every thought, every feeling, as if silence caused every step and gave rise to every action.

But even the afterglow is at some point almost or completely forgotten again. What remains is our sense of the discrepancy between the way we used to know how we were connected to reality and the manner in which we face reality again now.

Provided that we do not cling to the beautiful memory and painful regret, it is from the pain of this friction that the impulse arises to take in hand the search for silence. Not that we think we can recreate the happiness but rather because we feel that we can contribute our practice to it.

Does **the practice of silence** then simply serve our personal happiness? Some would say: how wonderful! What could be better than enjoying our happiness, since the world around us is in such a bad way? Others might reply: how egotistical and superficial! Do we human beings have no higher task on earth? But those who practise silence experience more and more clearly that life's task is realised in the breath enjoyed with gratitude;

that when we experience pure being, a consciousness responds to the gift of being. This consciousness has nothing to do with rational understanding. But it is still consciousness; therefore it has nothing in common either with a self-indulgent intoxication of the senses and even less can it be compared with a regression to some nebulous pre-natal harmony.

What takes place when we experience pure being cannot be put into words. Nevertheless, when, despite this knowledge, words do draw near to the ineffable, they might say: BEING recognises itself in the awareness of being of those who go beyond their differentiating consciousness by making room for silence within themselves.

From this dwelling place, from the place where silence enters, an effect emerges which goes beyond the practitioners, without any missionary effort on their part. They may come to understand, however, that from the beginning a deeper intent has been part of their longing for silence, which at first seemed so self-centred, and that their journey does not end with the experience of their own happiness and the creativity associated with it.

In contrast to egocentric satisfaction which does not care for others, this happiness of being is intrinsically connected with a growing sensibility for the suffering of those who feel they cannot follow this path, or of others who manage to cover up their need for silence with all kinds of substitute satisfactions and then have to suffer the consequences all the more severely. Coming from the experience of silence, the criteria for everyday action arise more and more from this fellow feeling and fellow being.

When, with time, an openness to silence becomes a component of whatever we do, we grow more sensitive to and respectful of every moment. The way we act may then gradually change, to our own benefit and for the well-being of others.

**Finding silence – but how?** By being silent, of course. It sounds so obvious, not to say trivial but hardly any of us realise it. Although outwardly we do: when we go in search of silence, we look for a silent place, in the woods or in the mountains. And it often happens that the wood or the mountain communicates its silence in such a way that we are enfolded and touched by it. But if we want to live from silence, it is good to create a silent place within ourselves; that is, to let ourselves be silent. It is exactly that, however, which is difficult to understand. Even in meditation we prefer to seek strenuous inner activity, instead of for once really letting ourselves be silent; as if that could not possibly be enough to reach the very depths.

It is as if in the end we do not really want to pay the price of giving up our controlling consciousness with which we constantly reassure ourselves that we are still exactly as we know ourselves to be. We fear death precisely where we sense new, true life.

However, we may also sense or fear that, by withdrawing active mental power, by truly descending into the depths, intermediate layers may become apparent which up to now we have preferred to ignore. In other words: we sense that the more we wake up to being who we truly are, the more we also wake up to the non-being we continue to be. When sitting in silence becomes our practice, the point is to attend to these shadow aspects too. Gone are the times when we thought that we could sweepingly dismiss and ignore as deceptive trivialities all the images and emotions which arise in meditation.

It is impossible to predict how gentle or dramatic the struggle with repressed pains or desires is going to be; that of course depends on the work we have already done on our consciousness in other ways. If appropriate, and if our experience of silence suggests it, we might look for additional healing options.

**Elements of sitting in silence**: Sitting in silence consists of remaining motionless for a period of time in a posture which is as relaxed as possible while also being alert (see the text on posture in the chapter 'Guidance on practice') and in focusing one's senses on a single thing. Only two of various possible starting points have been considered in this book: attending to the breath (see for this 'Picturing the flow of breath' in the chapter 'Guidance on practice') and attending to the awareness of silence itself.

**How do we live from silence?**
I do not know. There is no recipe for how to live from silence. We should beware of rigid intentions. But tried and tested prompts for practice and accounts of others' experiences can wake the sensibility of readers and foster their trust in their own way of practice. Any other 'hows' can be found in the texts of 'In the midst of it'.

Almost all the texts in this book emerged through contact with practitioners; that is, they were uttered spontaneously in a given situation and put down on paper afterwards. A number of changes naturally resulted when they were adapted for the written version. When possible I have avoided the direct address, as I did in my book

'Living Silence', to allow readers the greatest possible inner space when absorbing the text.[2]

---

[2] Translators' note: in order to avoid 'one', which sounds stilted in English, we have preferred to translate the German 'man' as 'you' or 'we'.

# AT THE THRESHOLD OF THE DAY

# FOR THE FIRST TIME

You come to sit in silence
for the first time, or – as if for the first time.

You take your time to arrange the place
as is right for you.
Perhaps you light a candle,
but that is not a must.

You stand at the place you have prepared
and bow. What for?
You do it until the bow knows the answer.

In your own time you position
your legs and hands
and in your mind's eye,
with your eyes almost closed,
in your mind's eye, you picture the posture
in which you sit
and see if it wants rearrangement.
And you fill the posture
with your self.

And you look at your breath, as it goes and comes,
and let the looking accompany the breath,
as it comes and goes.

And you let your breath listen to the silence,
how at some point it is there, for the first time.

How silence is there and always has been.
How silence always is,
as though it were the first time.

# BEGINNER

Some people do not want
to be beginners
at anything whatever,
at any price.

That is a pity.
For a beginner is
like a child.

Full of trust
and without suspicion,
a child begins
and looks at
what is becoming.

## LIKE A MOUNTAIN

How do we find a good mental and physical posture
for this sitting in silence?
The best way is to sit like a mountain.

At its base it is broad, the mountain.
It cedes its whole weight to the ground.
We need not make ourselves broader than we are.
It is enough to feel
how we earth ourselves in the ground
with the whole of our breadth
and the whole of our weight.

Higher up, the mountain narrows.
Its strength to soar
high and steep
grows out of the breadth at its base.
We need not strain beyond our height.
Bound as we are to the earth,
it is enough to straighten our back
until our awareness reaches upwards
from the crown of our head
to the space above,
towards the sky.

It is best to sit like a mountain
which looks out into the distance
with its breadth and height.
To do so, we need not keep our eyes wide open.
Like a mountain, we can look
with our whole posture.

It can see as far as the horizon,
letting happen
what is going on around it,
letting happen
what is coming to fruition in itself.

Like a mountain
which has gathered itself into itself
right from the horizon,
so that everything it sees and hears,
senses, feels and lives,
finds itself within it,
moment by moment.

Like a mountain
in which all experience joins together,
that of just now
and that of decades
and millennia ago,
in which both the joyful and the sorrowful
slowly crystallise of their own accord.

Like a mountain
which, completely still,
rests in itself,
in its bond
with earth and sky,
with nature and creatures,
with everything that is.

It is best
to sit there
like a mountain
which is simply there.

# SILENCE

Silence is always there,
from the innermost place
to the far horizon,
from the horizon
to the innermost place.

To become aware of it
is a question of practice.
If we become aware of it,
it is like a miracle.

It is like a miracle
that we ourselves are then
nothing but
this silence,
from the innermost place
to the far horizon.

Nothing but
this silence,
as we
just sit here,
just like this.

# LETTING YOURSELF ARRIVE

Taking your time to arrive,
to arrive in this room,
in this place of silence.

Taking your time to arrive
in awareness of the ground.
Perhaps tension is released here or there
into the silent ground.

Taking your time, too, to arrive,
sensing your connection to the space around you,
up to the space above your head,
up to the silent space there.

Watching how breath flows
towards the ground,
how breath rises out of the silence.

Watching how breath breathes
towards the distant horizon,
how the distance breathes towards you.

And whatever else comes to the surface,
whether welcome or not,
you see it surface and let it sink,
you take note of it and pay no heed.

You watch again and again and always anew,
how it breathes into the silence, out,
and breathes from the silence, in.
How silence breathes, out and in.

## A MAYFLY

You sit and take your time,
time to be there,
to be there, alert in the silence,
without paying attention to anything
except the silence.

And it is going quite well;
but at some point,
perhaps because it is going quite well,
at some point something slackens.
All at once you are simply dozing.

Since it was going quite well, you
forgot what you were about,
as happens in life,
and when you notice it,
it is no longer going well at all.

Perhaps it would be enough, then,
to think of yourself as a mayfly,
in order to treat this day
as if it stood for the whole of your life,

and in order once more to surrender yourself,
completely awake, to this moment,
in order to take this whole silence
and fill it wholly with yourself.

# CENTRE AND DISTANCE

How can we best
keep ourselves centred?

We can stretch our own silence
as far as the horizon
and let ourselves be held in our centre
by this wide space.

We can then breathe out
in all directions into the space,
we can then breathe in
from all directions into the centre.

With time we can observe
how space itself breathes.

With time we can see
how space itself observes.

So we need only stretch
our silence
or non-silence
as far as the horizon,
and let it
place us into the centre.
Into the centre of everything.
Into the centre of now.

## ALL RIGHT

Silence becomes perceptible only
if we are ready for it,
that means
when we are not preoccupied
with grumbling about
ourselves and our situation.

Everyone knows this of course.
But it is quite another thing
to realise emotionally
that right now,
just as we are sitting here,
we are perfectly all right.

To realise emotionally
that everything
that is part of our present situation,
that all of it
is part of our being all right.

Silence only becomes perceptible
if we are ready
to feel a dimension of all-rightness
which our understanding cannot grasp.

Silence is
when what always is
is perfectly all right.

# EXPECTING

Sitting in silence
we should not expect anything.
But we naturally hope
for a deeper recognition of who
we really are;

for an ever deeper
and broader experience of silence
and thus of being one;
for an ever new
becoming whole and complete
out of this being one.

We should not expect nothing.
But we should not disturb the silence
by wanting
what we most fervently expect.

## IN EXPECTATION

Sitting in silence
is like waiting expectantly
until the silent expectation
melds
with the expected silence.

Until, in this in-breath,
silence is born
from silence.

Until, in this out-breath,
silence fades
into silence.

## READINESS

This readiness
to become empty,

this readiness
to let come,

this readiness
to begin from the beginning,

this readiness –
that is practice.

# SPECTATOR

How does it happen, that
although we really seek silence,
all at once idle scraps of thought
drown it out?

It is best
not to be interested
in this question.

When it happens,
it is best
to imagine sitting
as if behind ourselves
and to take note of
the phenomenon of thoughts
from a quiet distance.

Sometimes it is as though
they were pulling us outwards
in a thousand directions,
all over the place.

Sometimes it is
as though they were pulling us deep downwards,
deeply and heavily.

Sometimes it is
as though they were pulling us into ourselves,
dark, cramped.

Sometimes it is also
as though the thoughts were pulling us up and away,
just away and away.

But we remain
in the place behind ourselves
and, like spectators at the theatre,
observe what is acting and pulling
on the stage of our thoughts.

However alertly the spectators watch,
they are not pulled along
in any direction.

It is silent where they sit.
And at some point
they wonder
where the thought actors
have moved on to.

# I DO NOT KNOW

Letting ourselves arrive
in this place
where we are now sitting.
Letting ourselves arrive now.

Now – those are my feet
which touch the ground – here.
Now – those are my hands
which lie inside each other – here.
Now – those are my ears
which listen to the silence – here.

Now – this breathing.
Now – the silence.
Now – I do not know.

# COMPLETE

Again and again,
letting myself arrive in this room,
in this place,
in this body, in this breathing.

Letting myself arrive in this silence,
in this complete silence.

What? You think the silence is not yet complete?
Some tension here, an uneasy feeling there,
there a thought and then a hundred more.

What? You think the silence is not yet complete,
as long as this and that is not
as you imagine silence to be?
Silence is not as you imagine it.
Silence is when everything is allowed to be
exactly as it is now,
with this tension,
with the uneasy feeling,
with this thought and a hundred more.

If we let everything be,
completely be
just as it is,
then silence is complete
of its own accord.

You do not believe it?
Then don't!
Let yourselves be!
But right now.

## FORCING THE BREATH

Some people
have become so used to
putting pressure on themselves
that they cannot stop
doing so
even when sitting in silence.

They push
and force their breath
as if they
were unable to live
without this breath pressure.

Nevertheless, they should
try out just once
what it is like
not to force their breath.

Most likely they will be able
to breathe a sigh of relief
and live.

## MUST AND CANNOT

In the middle of the silence
it occurs
to some people
to think
they must.
They must
do or be or stop something;
there is something they must.

And straight away they think,
even before they have any idea
what it could be about,
straight away they think
they cannot;
that this is asking too much.

Much too much was probably asked of them
a long while ago
and the experience
has led them to form
a fixed idea of themselves.

Sitting in silence,
when old Must and Cannot
stand in the way of silence yet again,
then you can regard old Must and Cannot
as something obsolete,
so that by leaving them behind you see anew:
just now I must nothing,
just now I can
breathe,
live,
be.

# DIFFICULT

If, for whatever reason,
our practice becomes difficult,
we instinctively tend
either to battle
against the difficulty
or inwardly to run away
from the practice.

But the practice
is no less effective
when it appears to be difficult.

We could remember,
remember with trust,
that difficult moments
or phases
belong to the practice,
to our own practice too,
our own, just now.

## NOT CALCULATING

If pain
gets worse,
we are inclined
to calculate
how this torment
might have increased
by the end of the sit.

And we wonder
whether we will,
and want to, bear it.

But when sitting in silence,
pain
is quite unpredictable.
Just as it arises
out of the blue,
so can it unexpectedly
disappear.

So we should
neither fear
nor hope
but, with or without pain,
just sit here in silence
right now.

## CHOP OR SKEDADDLE

It often happens,
and you do not always know why,
that, when sitting in silence, at first
your thoughts rush hither and thither
out of control.

Some instructions for sitting
in silence say
you should simply cut off your thoughts:
chop!
Other instructions say
you should observe them carefully: like this, this, this!
Yet others say
you should simply let them run: skedaddle!

Which will you follow?
I do not know.
Sometimes I say cut them off: chop!
Sometimes I say watch: like this, this, this.
Sometimes I say let them run: skedaddle!

But this morning I say:
let yourselves arrive here
at this, your place,
in your silence.

Let yourselves notice
how you touch the silent ground
with your sitting

and how your posture
makes a connection
with the silent space
above your head

and how your own form
is surrounded
by wide silent space.

Let yourselves notice
how your breath glides,
how your silence flows.

Let thoughts mingle in
if they want to.
Keep silent,
be friendly to them.

# SUFFERING

Who would not like to overcome suffering?

It is said that sages
have overcome suffering,
suffering from all kinds of pain.

And therefore they have overcome fear,
the fear of suffering,
and they have overcome the need to fend off,
fend off suffering.

How did they get there?
It is said they realise
that every manifestation and perception
is of the One Unconditioned being.[1]

How did they get to
this realisation?
It is said that in their practice of being silent
they reach this realisation.

By letting themselves fall silent,
by letting all their knowing
and comprehending and wanting
fall silent,
letting all their wishing
and fearing
fall silent,
letting all imagining and pondering
fall silent.

---

[1] See footnote on page iv.

By letting themselves fall silent in this way,
they surrender themselves to the wisdom
which makes itself known in silence,
invariably,
inevitably.

And what does this wisdom
proclaim?
It says, in one way or another
it says:
all manifestation and perception is
of the One Unconditioned
and whole being.

The broken, too, is
of the whole being.

Everything is, just as it is,
this whole being.

You yourself are, just as you are,
of this One being.

Your breathing in, your breathing out,
your now is
of the one whole enduring being.

## OLD DISCONTENTS

When silence wants to arise in us,
it often brings up not only
itself, silence,
but, however contradictory it might seem,

sometimes it also brings up moods
and discontents
which we quietened long ago,
so that they have been able to remain hidden
for months and years,
so that they have kept quiet,
as though they were part of our silence.

But as it arises,
true silence brings up
what has been hidden
and then the unwanted moods, for their part,
immediately cover up
the rising silence again.

What can we do?
We cannot do anything.
It is enough
to see and to respect
the discontents,
even though we thought they were long-since forgotten.
It is enough
not to despise ourselves because of them.

The sooner we assent
to what has been
and to how we still feel,
the sooner silence enters
and changes what we feel
and opens our eyes to what
wants to become of it.

## PROCESSING

Sitting in silence,
we would sometimes quite like
to process in some way
what
went on with us yesterday.

And so, quite automatically,
we tend to
follow the thoughts
which relate to it.

Doing this, we forget
that in our own silence
the deepest processing happens
of its own accord.

We forget
that it is enough
for yesterday's and tomorrow's sake
to go into the now.

# PEACE

Sitting in silence
you should simply
let yourself fully arrive.
Let yourself fully arrive
in the peace
of this moment.

How can you actually do that,
let yourself arrive in peace,
given there are so many people
who tragically
have to suffer
from the lack of peace in the world?
Given there are so many people
who, in one way or another,
find themselves
in overwhelming need
and unspeakable suffering?

Can it do them good
if – with them in mind –
others
let themselves arrive
in the peace
of this moment?

## TO WHAT END?

Just when the practice
seems laborious
and you do not really know
what purpose it might
actually still serve,
just then,
you might remember
a deep stirring
in your soul,
a stirring
which says, right at the beginning
of all practising:
I really want
my practice-on-myself
to serve the well-being
of all forms of life,
just as I
have gratefully experienced,
or merely surmise,
that the practice
of my teachers
and all the great sages
has served and still serves
my own development.

## WHAT FOR?

Some people practise sitting in silence
in order to advance so far
that one day they will make no more mistakes.
You laugh?
But some people are like that.

And some people practise sitting in silence,
in order to fulfil a necessary daily duty,
like cleaning their teeth or paying bills.
You laugh?
But some people are like that.

Some people practise sitting in silence
in order to protect themselves from the trials of everyday
life
or to arm themselves against them.
You laugh?
But some people are like that.

Some people practise sitting in silence
in order to be as composed as their teachers.
You laugh?
But some people are like that.

Some people practise sitting in silence
in order to experience
very great enlightenment one day.
You laugh?
But some people are like that.

Some people practise sitting in silence
and do not know what they do it for.
They simply sit in silence.

## WHERE TO?

Where does this sitting in silence
actually lead us?
Does it lead us to ourselves?
Does it lead us to the other?
So how would we like it?

Absurd question!
Have we not long since experienced
how silence pushes us
towards ourselves,
towards this self
which cannot be equated
with the changing sensations,
thoughts and feelings
which we think of as being us
while we flee from ourselves.

Do we not remember
how silence draws us
to the self
which in itself
is like pure silence,
like nothing,
like nothing but silence;

and have we not seen
how it is precisely this experience
which opens us to the other?
As if in the other and in me there were
only this one silent self
only this one silence itself.

## NOT-THINKING

Sitting in silence
is a way
to enter
a state of mind
in which we rest
in the space of the unconditioned.

If we have found
such a state,
we recognise
that we have always
rested in this space
of the unconditioned.

But how can we
reach this state?
Just now the best
we can do is
not to think about it.

Then what?
Really, the best we can do now
is not-thinking.

Not-thinking is an action.
You do not believe it?
Then you are not yet doing it.
No sooner do you do it,
not-thinking,
than resting in the space of the unconditioned
takes place.

## BECOMING STUPID

Sometimes I really fear that I am becoming stupid
when I devote myself to not-thinking.

If I then look closer,
if, from a position of not-thinking, I look out,
I see how this very fear
is nothing but an unusual fruit
of my habitual unmindful thinking.

How odd: my unbiased not-thinking
clearly recognises the bias of my thinking.

And then what?
What do I do then?
There it is again!
Again the old thought-track,
the 'then-what' brake,
which wants to stop
the natural process of this recognition,

as if it could not be, as if it were forbidden
that not-thinking should lead on further,
beyond the threatening loss of
thought patterns,
right through thought-silence,
to the creative idea
which, out of what has never been thought,
sows seed onto the fallow now.

So once again I engage with
the silence of not-thinking,
engage with
this mysterious NOT.

# INSIGHT

Seen with the eyes of everyday consciousness,
a change for the better takes place
when we gain insight
into our opinions,
steered as they are by desire and fear,
and thus also into the one-sidedness of our behaviour.

For when we identify with our own wishes,
we do not see the need of others.
Those who understand this will try
to let go of this fixation
and be more available to others.

Sitting in silence
is also about insight.
But almost the other way round:
we practise
in order to look into the silence
and thus into our bond
with all that is
and with all who are with us.

Identification with what is ours
then dissolves of its own accord
through contemplating
how we are bound together.

The practice is
to contemplate
the silence.

# RECUPERATION

Sitting in silence is recuperation.
For by entrusting ourselves so completely to the silence
through our familiar practice,
we release
our habitual idea of ourselves
into the silence
and in this way
strength arises
from our intrinsic knowledge,
from the sense of
how we are meant to be,
from our enduring knowledge
of who we really are.

By entrusting ourselves
so completely to the silence,
we let go of
how we have become
and so strength arises
out of not-having-become.

Thus sitting in silence
is to fetch ourselves anew
from the heart of silence.

We do not have to
concern ourselves with this.
It is enough
to entrust ourselves completely
to the silence
through our familiar practice.

# OUT

Sitting in silence is,
of course, a kind of withdrawal,
at first anyway.

We withdraw from
what we are clinging and sticking to just now,
we withdraw from ourselves.

Some people think
that in doing this they should
somehow make themselves smaller
than they are
and so they pull in their heads
until, or so they imagine,
until they are invisible.

But that is not the aim of the practice.
Perhaps this very day
it is time
to expose yourself to the silence
in your full natural size.
Perhaps just now
it is time
to pull away the veil you hide behind
and to step out, upright and breathing.

Not in order to win or to shine,
only to step out
so that you yourself take part
in the just now.

## SMILING

Sitting in silence
is a serious matter.
Focusing our senses
on our breath
demands earnest engagement,
otherwise we are
– and who doesn't know that –
otherwise we are soon lost
in thoughts about this and that.

But seriousness should
not darken our countenance
until it takes on a dismal expression of control.

Today, for example,
a merry smile
could also
go to meet the silence,
a smile
which widens our jaw bones,
which spreads up to our temples,
which sinks down as far as our pelvis,
a smile
which, coming from our heart,
meets the silence
merrily,
in utter seriousness.

## SLEEPING LONGER

Sometimes I, too, would
rather sleep longer
than brood in this silence.

My head
sits on my shoulders
as if I had no neck.

Breath crawls,
time drags.
Oh well.

Then at some point – how did that happen?
At some point
breath woke up.
Undeserved clarity !

I would never
prefer to sleep longer.

## PLAYING

Sometimes, like a small child,
I would rather
go and play
than sit in silence.

Then I play
the game of sitting in silence.

I play sitting solidly on the ground,
reaching deep down into the earth.
I play stretching up to the heights,
tall and light,
as if climbing above heavy clouds.

I play my game
of sitting in silence
and observe the flow of breath
which is playing in me.

I play
sailing along on this flow of breath,
in my ship.
My ship sails and sails,
it sails into the distance.

My ship sails and sails,
it sails into the silence.

My ship sails and sails,
it sails to me.

## CARNIVAL TIME

When sitting in silence
it is always carnival time.
Anyone who sits in silence
is a fool.

What is a fool like?
Mad and stupid?
No, a fool is free, has a fool's freedom.

Fools take the liberty
not to believe in their preconceived ideas
and thus to trust the moment.

They take the liberty
not to care
what others think of them.

They do not think
they must be
how they have become,
nor do they think
they should be different.

They take the liberty
to forget
what they know of themselves
and to sit there
as if they do not know themselves.

They are free from themselves
and are therefore one
with what is.

## LENT

Last week carnival.
Today Lent.
Now, too, it is fitting to sit in silence.

The Lenten practice is not to give in
to instinctive impulses, for a short while.
That is, not to think: I must!

In practice that means not giving in
when we think that we must scratch
because something itches.
In practice, that means not giving in
when we think we must cheer loudly
because we are glad
or wail because we are in pain.

In practice that means not giving in
when we think we must
follow our marvellous ideas
because we will otherwise forget them.

In practice that means
catching ourselves at every must-thought
or must-feeling
so that we can discover
how good it feels
not to follow the must.
How freely we sit here!
As if we were fools!
How wonderful it is
simply to return
to this breath.

# BIRTHDAY

I sit here in silence
on my birthday.

Is sitting in silence
today something special?
What a little child you are!

Coming from silence
is always birthday for me.

Yes, I am
like a little child.

## ALL SOULS

All Souls:
the day on which,
strictly speaking,
we remember all souls.

It is impossible to remember
all souls.
And in fact we mean
only the dead.
But we cannot remember
all the dead either.

Rather, we mean
those to whom we were personally attached.
Can we even remember all of them?

If we want to,
at the beginning of this silent time
we can call to mind
that countless dead are part of our lives,
that countless souls
have been engaged on our behalf,
whether we knew them or not,
that perhaps right now
countless dead are engaging with
our own development,
wishing us well.

If we want to,
we can then
open up
the space of our own silence,
as if we wanted to invite
these souls
to share in the silence today.

We can open ourselves
to the possible presence of these souls,
whether we remember
someone in particular
or whether we mean
the whole well-wishing
community of the dead.

In this silence,
we can then perhaps
reply with the feeling:
and I am sitting here
for you.

I want to engage with you
through my respectful,
grateful silence,
today and tomorrow.

## NON-HOLIDAY

All Saints and All Souls are over.
The feast days are over,
when, sitting in silence,
we were able
to open ourselves
to a special space,
almost without trying.
To the space of the saints
of the whole world.
To the space of those who have died,
near and far.

But today?
To what kind of space
should we open ourselves today,
on this unspecial day?

We could open ourselves to empty space
today, on this non-holiday,
to empty, empty space.
What? We do not want to?
Are we afraid?
Could we get lost in it?

If we turn
to the empty space,
in spite of our dread and with all our fear,
if we dare
to refrain from
secretly thinking
a small something into it
that we can hold onto,

if we dare
to open ourselves completely
to the empty space,
then it might be
that empty space reveals itself,
reveals that it itself
is the **one** empty space,

the one space
of all the saints,
the one space
of all the dead,
the one space
of all the living,
the one space
of all specks of dust,
the one abundant space,
the space
of my own self.

## PLANETS

Of course it is enough,
when sitting in silence,
simply to listen to the silence
and to accompany it with our breath.

But at the beginning of this silence
it could do us good, too,
to think once in a while of the seven planets,
how they circle round this place just now,
near or far away.

Then we could perhaps notice
that silent, gentle moonlight
flows around us
like a sheltering mantle.

Or, we could observe
Mercury, the mediator between heaven and earth,
coming and going
with our breath, almost unnoticed,
as if he took each out-breath with him into the heights
and from there brought fresh breeze
to us as we breathe in.

Or we could feel Venus sitting next to us
in her devotion,
as if she placed her selflessness onto the very spot
where we cannot yet
let ourselves go.

Or we could feel Martian strength
take hold of our posture,
strength to sit tall,
spurring us on: off you go!
Off to the finishing line,
off into the now!

Or we could hear Jupiter sounding
as if from far away,
out from the great space.
Yes, he sounds: yes you! Yes, yes!

And if at some point we
have lost ourselves
in thoughts and feelings and think
we will not get anywhere anyway,
then at last we might
see Saturn
full on, face to face.
Stay, is all he says.
Stay there! Stay with it! Stay now!

Oh – and the sun,
have we forgotten him?
Here he sits,
breathes in and out,
just taking in
how the other planets
circle round him.
The sun
breathes in and out,
the sun
breathes himself.

# DAYBREAK

To sit at daybreak
is a wonderful thing.
And at once we cling
to the wonderful.
Would it be better then
to sit at dusk?
That is wonderful too.
Better to cling
to the wonderful
than not to sit.

## FAMILIAR

Here we sit again
in the familiar room,
in the familiar place.
Here, once again, is
the familiar connection to the ground.
And, higher up,
this familiar connection
to the space above our heads.
Familiar connection, too,
to the space around us.
To the people and – or –
to the things in the room.
At the same time familiar
sitting-alone,
completely by and for ourselves.

Familiar breathing.
Familiar silence.
Familiar space.
Familiar scraps of thought.
Familiar feelings.
Familiar disturbance.
Familiar pain.
Familiar being familiar.
Familiar right now.

## NOW AND TIME

Some people imagine
NOW to be a short piece of time,
a very short piece,
between what was
and what is not yet.

But in our experience
NOW is
not a part of anything.
In our experience
NOW is
whole
and therefore so infinitely vast
that it contains everything
that has been and is to come.

At the same time,
in our experience
NOW is not somehow blurred.
It is as clearly outlined
as the fibre of the carpet in front of us.
It is as unique
as the high-pitched sound of birds in spring.
It is as precise
as the fine point of contact
between our own thumbs here.
As we experience it,
this small point where they touch
is the entire NOW.

# NOW

If we have already practised
sitting in silence many times,
we can easily think
we already know silence
and know
what this encounter might be like.
That is a pity.
For by thinking this,
we close ourselves to
the unimagined new possibility
of this particular day.

It could be
completely different today;
What would that be like?

But it could also be
that today
I shall experience a single moment
as really now,
whether it resembles yesterday's or not.
What will that be like?

## NO TIME

Sitting down into silence
as if there were no time.
As if we did not know
whether it was morning
or evening.

As if there were no time.
No before,
no after,
no now,
only this
always.

## MISSING SILENCE

If we enjoy silence,
we should be happy about it.

If we miss silence,
well – then I do not know either.

Is it even possible to miss silence?

If we fail to notice it,
it is because
we are busy
with something else
and do not see
that we are missing silence.

But if we miss it,
is it not already almost here?
When we long for it,
is it not already coming towards us?
What is it like now?

## HABIT

With silence it is
the same as with other things.

To begin with there is great enthusiasm
but then it gives way to habit.

At some point we know it, the silence.
What else could it give us?

Real sitting in silence begins
when we go beyond habit
and bring ourselves into it
from moment to moment,
in order to discover anew and more deeply
what is and what that is like,
and in order
to discover
how what is imperfect, like yesterday,
is at the same time
perfect,
and always has been.

# RED SKY IN THE MORNING

With silence it is the same as with a red morning sky.
Sometimes the eastern sky lights up
with a gentle, golden red.
At some point, and we cannot grasp the moment,
this special glow gives way to daylight
in which the usual contours
emerge once again.

But if we want to, we can always
remind ourselves of it during the day
and then, for a short while, it will be
as though we were seeing this special light again.

So too, the light of silence
which from time to time gently shines into our practice,
gradually fades
after we stand up
and gives way to the usual contours
of our everyday way of seeing.

But whenever we want to,
we can remind ourselves of
silence
and immediately we see everyday things
and problems,
and also ourselves, in the other light.

So it dawns on us,
morning-dawns on us quite gradually,
who we really are, all of us,
we living beings and we things.

But for now we should look for nothing else
but silence in this sitting here.

## AS WITH A PLANT

With silence it is the same as with a plant.
If you have a plant at home
and do not water it,
it withers.

If you water it every day,
it lives
but you should not expect
it to flower every day.

If you look at it day by day,
you do not even see
that it is growing.

It should be enough for you to see
that it is there.
And from time to time you will feel
that it means something to you,
that it has an effect on you.

If you are lucky,
it sometimes comes into flower
and bears visible fruit.

It is the same with silence,
which lives within us like a plant.
If you do not tend the silence
by sitting,
it appears to dry up.

But if you practise daily,
you should not expect
it to flower
or to bear fruit every day.

If you look day by day,
you do not even see
that it is growing.

It should be enough for you to trust
that it is with you.
From time to time you will know
that this sitting means something to you
and that the silence has an effect on you.

If you are lucky,
the silence may also blossom some time
into a deep experience
and bear visible fruit.

But the singular nature of silence is
that it also bears fruit in those
who do not experience the blossoming
and do not know about the fruit.
Perhaps only others savour it.
Then the meaning of sitting is all the more fulfilled.

So how do you take care of silence?
By pouring yourself out again and again,
keeping quiet,
as now.

## WHY NOT

Why can we not
remain all day
sitting like this
in silence?

We can
walk
all day
with silence.

# IN THE MIDST OF IT

## In the midst of it – Steps

### IS IT THIS?

Coming out of silence
I walk again,
a few steps.

Enquiring
attentiveness
walks with me.

'Is it this?'
it asks
step by step.

Step by step
is the answer:
step
by step.

### THIS STEP

My now
is this step.
While I
walk on
further
and further,
this one step
remains my now.

## EYES AND LEGS

Silence,
although it
is completely still,
silence
has eyes
and legs.

What is it like
when silence itself
walks and looks?


## MOUNTAIN, GRASS AND COW

Coming out of silence
I go outside,
see mountain,
grass
and cow.

But suddenly
I realise
how all I see
lets me
be.

And my eyes, too,
let
mountain,
grass
and cow be.

## WALKING IN THE MIST

What does it really do,
this thick mist?

Does it take
the last remnant
of clear vision from us?

Or, with its soft light,
does it
unite what seems to us
impossible to join together?

Walking in the mist.

## GOLDEN AUTUMN WIND

The golden autumn wind
is a wonderful thing.
A pity
that we never see it.

We can only sense
that it is the wind,
when golden leaves fly
through the air,

when people in the street
hold on to their hats,

when a gust blows right
into our faces, whoosh!

The golden autumn wind,
does it need anything or anyone
to attest to itself?

The golden autumn wind,
does it need our seeing,
to show itself?

It needs our walking
in the golden autumn wind.

## SNOW

The deep snow
leaves
hardly any paths open.
And so snow-deep silence
compels me
to take only
this small step
up the path,
and down.

## EASY

Walking along
it occurs to me
that I could
also take my steps
as if everything
were very easy.

At least
I could find out
whether there is not something easy
walking with me!

## *In the midst of it – Pausing*

### WHAT IS REAL

When we truly practise,
we seek and hope
to meet and recognise
what is real,
wherever we may
stand or walk.

Who shows us
what is real?
Vegetables,
the stair landing,
the window.

How can we see it?
We cannot see it.
But what is real within us
sees and sees.

## WE CANNOT MISS IT

If we trust,
we cannot miss It.
In fact, there is no way
of ever missing It.

Only
if we trust
do we know this.

## RESPONSIBLE

What is happening to me
right now
is not
in my control.

And yet
I myself bear
full responsibility
for what
happens to me.

I am
responsible
for right now.

How can I be?
I do not know.
I am.


## BAD

In the midst of it,
out of the blue,
it crosses
my mind:

I could never be
as bad
as I see myself just now!

# THERE IT IS AGAIN

There it is again, this:
not yet!

In the midst of it,
in a harmless pause,
in keeping silent for a moment:

a dark 'not-yet!'
'still not yet!'

Really?
What glows there,
in that pausing
and remaining
in the midst of not-yet?

Brightly glows
the light
of the dark
not-yet.

## BAD THINGS

Some things are simply
too bad
to look at.

But if we make it our practice,
to look at them anyway,

if we simply do not stop
looking at them,

as if the bad things wanted
nothing more
than that we should look at them
right to the end,

it might happen,
that they mysteriously
change within ourselves

and that we ourselves are then
transformed
by these changed things.

## PAIN

What is this about?
All of a sudden a pain
right in my heart.

Do I want to know?
I know it straight away.
Yes, I regret
what I did
to you or to you.

Oh, I wish
it had not
happened like that,
that it had not
been me.

But it happened.
It was me.

I wish –
or do I already see it approach?
I wish the opportunity were here
for me to restore
what can be set right.

Any remaining pain
I shall bear
with dignity.

WHY?

How often do we ask ourselves:
Why?
Why is it as it is?
Why?
Why does it have to be like this?

Only when it grows silent,
then everything is
without a why.

In silence, light as well as darkness
finds its way home
into the mystery of itself.

And no-one asks:
Why is it silent
just now?

## WONDERFUL NOW

The wonderful thing about now is
that, whatever it may be like,
there is nothing about it
to find fault with.

When we ourselves
become now,
then there is no crack
between anything and ourselves,
no crack
leaving room
for a fault.

Wonderful now!

## THE GATES OF TRUTH

It is said in the wisdom texts
that the gates of truth
are innumerable.

Innumerable chances
to see,
to hear,
to experience
true reality?

I know only one gate:
this moment now.
This breath.

## TRAFFIC LIGHT

Red light,
pause,
keep silent.

Acute
attention
inwards,
outwards,
towards neither nor.

Intense
silence.
Green light,
Go!

## WHAT CONCERNS ME

Hardly have I paused
than I sense,
no,
I know,
what truly concerns me
right now,
what wants to engage
with me.

So I go along
and concern myself with it.

*In the midst of it – Acting*

GET UP!

Sometimes
I would feel so utterly well
sitting in silence

that one day
I asked my teacher
why I could not
simply remain sitting
all day long,
– at least just for the days
of sesshin.[2]

His reply was:
let go of this thought
and get up!

---

[2] retreat

# LAUGHTER

Having got up
from sitting in silence
I am overcome
by laughter,
laughter and more laughter.

Not that there is anything to laugh about.
Groundlessly
it laughs
and laughs
from the soul's
deep ground.

Going further,
my laughter sees
how every single thing
meets me with laughter.
Umbrella stands, wall and shoe.
Not that there is anything to laugh about.
Groundlessly
each thing
laughs,
laughs
from the deep
ground of being.

## PLAYTIME

Work time
is not playtime.
Only for small children
there is no difference.
When they clean vegetables,
they play cleaning vegetables.
When they garden,
they play gardening.
And doing so
they quite forget themselves.
Then they are vegetable cleaners,
then they are gardeners.
In this way they are whole –
wholly themselves.
And they are even
having fun doing it,
the children.

## BEING PRESENT

Usually, when we do some simple task,
our mind is not on it,
our thoughts wander
here and there;
we are not in this work,
are not present.

It is not that this is bad.
It is only a pity
because then we receive nothing
from what we are actually doing.
Because then
we do not experience being present.

What could we receive
from shovelling snow
or peeling carrots?

Well, if we do not feel it is too
lowly and ordinary
to devote ourselves
completely
to shovelling snow,
to peeling carrots,
or whatever we have to do,
then we are able to experience
what this work is giving us
and then we might experience
how fulfilling
this being present is.

## ATTENDING

How about
doing this work,
without thinking
of better
or worse,
of faster
or slower,
without thinking
of exciting
or boring?

How about
doing this work
simply attending
to each movement,
attending to each movement
as if it were the whole of life,
as if it were life itself?

# BEING WHOLLY PRESENT

Sometimes
being-wholly-present
happens just
when we inwardly
withdraw a little from
what we are doing.

Withdraw
from concentrating too hard
and striving too much.

As if doing
happened of its own accord.
As if being-wholly-present
happened
of its own accord.

## BRIDGE

How can I ever find
a bridge
to being still
in everyday activity?

A bridge
between the movement
I make
and awareness
of the motionless?

I entrust
the awareness
of the motionless
to the movement.

In this way I am
the bridge myself.

# COLLECTING STILLNESS

How can
we collect ourselves
in stillness
while we work?

Feet collect
stillness in walking,

hands collect
stillness in doing.

The eye collects
stillness in seeing.

## EVEN MORE SILENT

Could this activity
right now
become
even more silent?

I do not mean
we should take care
to make less noise.

I mean the delicate interest
in how silence can intensify
and spread out
in every daily activity.

I mean the interest
in the effect
of activity growing
more and more silent,
in how that affects
the actor.

And in the effect
it has on the things
acted on in silence.

Could it become even more silent?

## BEING REALLY SILENT

How can we recognise
whether we are really silent?
We recognise it
by all things
meeting us in silence.

## PRESENT

Simply being present
in what
we are doing.

Forgetting ourselves
into
being present.

Until we wake up
in the doing.

# RESPONSIBILITY

The more we wake to ourselves,
the more responsible we feel
for the space
in which we happen to be
and for the things
which have been entrusted to us
for our work.

Therefore it is enough
to wake to ourselves
while we clean and wash the dishes
or weed and rake the garden
or formulate thoughts and write,
or while we do whatever it is
we are doing.

It is always enough,
to wake completely to ourselves
and be responsible.

## EVERYDAY IS THE WAY

The old masters say:
'everyday is the way.'
Some people
understand by this
that we should
follow our inward practice
in everyday life as well.

But that is not
what the old masters say.
They say:
'everyday **is** the way'.

Then how could we
fear that the everyday
could lead us off the way?

Everyday itself
is itself the way.

This everyday moment of mine,
only it,
is the way.

## EVERY ACTION

Every action
I take
connects with
millions of movements
which have led to it
and with millions of movements
which arise from it.

Yet this movement here,
at this moment,
is the only action
in the whole universe.
Without a before
without an after.

*In the midst of it – Pausing again*

## ENLIGHTENMENT

What enlightenment makes us realise
is
that not only
this moment
is perfect,
but that
our whole life
as it was
was perfect.

That nothing has been lacking,
whatever it was
we have missed.

Why not
recognise
at this moment
that the now
lacks nothing?

## THEN

My now is now.
This standing here.
This drawing breath.
This thought
of then.
Now.

I

Sometimes
when I think of my mother
and with my mind's eye see her before me,
I see
how I resemble her,
although she was
so completely different
from me.

Sometimes
when I think of my father,
I feel just the same,
even though he was
in even greater measure
different
from me.

Sometimes
when I meet my brother,
I see
how we resemble each other,
even though
I am so completely different
from him.

Sometimes
when I pass a stranger
on the road,
I do not think
we resemble each other,

and yet I feel
that I am
encountering
a ME.

Sometimes
when I observe a sparrow
or a dog,
then, too,
I see
this ME.

When I
look at a tree
or a stone
or a lampshade
then –
yes, even then, it appears,
unexpectedly,
this I.

But always
when I look into the silence,
the silence sees ITSELF.

# FREE TIME

Suddenly some free time.
An hour
of free time.

Free time!
How is time free?
How am I free?

Is my standing here free?
This movement,
is it free?

The houses over there,
are the houses free?

And the mountains?
And the bird?

And my looking,
is my looking free?

Another half hour
of free time.

## STUPID

As I pause,
it has only just grown quiet
when it comes back to me
how stupidly
I behaved
just now.

How I stood there
so stupidly.
And everyone now knows –
how stupid!

I stop in my tracks
and want to
run away.
Really?

I stay
and look,
look and look,
breathing out,
breathing in,
look and look.

I sense
already:
stupid
is stupid
and stupid is
not stupid.
Everything is fine.
I walk on.

## ANGER

There is always something
to get angry about!
Before me I see him
or her or all of those
who have just made me angry!
These – oh, just drop it!
Better to look at myself,
observe
how angry I am.
I see myself before me:
is that me?
See myself –
it's me.
Suddenly, peacefully, I see
him or her or all those
I thought
had made me angry,
see them with me.

## LOOKING INTO

Pausing
to look into
the nature of my self
for a moment.

Standing and looking,
I am aware of my feet
and it is as if the feet
were looking into
the nature of their selves.

I am aware of my looking
and it is
as if my looking were looking
into
the nature of its self.

I walk on
and it is
as if looking
itself were walking.

## UGLY STAIN

If we take time
for the span of a breath
to become aware
of the expanse
around us,
the expanse
all the way to the horizon,
then it may happen
that we
find
an equal expanse again
in the little radish
on the plate,
or in the pencil
in the hand,
or in the small ugly stain
on the trousers.

## PROMPT

Sometimes
when I pause,
I am astonished
that a small prompt
I once
received for my practice
has actually
had some effect.

Then, when I
look more closely
at how it happened,
it usually has to do with the fact
that I actually
followed
that prompt.

## FAILING TO CATCH THE SILENCE

Some people
are afraid
they will miss
the silence.
And so they do miss it,
the silence.

How can we avoid
missing it?
We cannot
miss it.

## RAIN AND WIND

Pausing,
I look
out of the window.
How is it
that the flow of my breath
all at once melds
with the sound of the rain,
with the swinging
of the branches in the wind?
As if the rain breathed.
Or does the wind rock me?

## MAY NO-ONE BE FORGETFUL

May no-one forget
to become aware
when a flower blooms,
when a door bangs,
when the wind whistles,
when a now is.

# AT THE THRESHOLD
# OF THE NIGHT

## WAKING TO YOURSELF

At the end of the day:
Time to sit in silence.
Time to awake.
Time to be with yourself.
Time to stay with yourself.
Time to begin anew,
no matter how long you have practised already.

How do you do that,
wake to yourself?

You look
at the person
you want to wake to,
at yourself.

Looking at yourself,
how you sit here
and breathe
and keep silent.

You are already awake to yourself.
Nothing else is needed.

## SIMPLE

Sitting in silence means
simply sitting here in silence
and breathing,
letting yourself be.

What is difficult
about this sitting in silence is
that it is so simple.

So simple that you keep thinking
it cannot possibly be so simple,
something else is needed;

and therefore you do not
stay with what is simple,
so what is simple
can hardly grow deeper.

What does it mean to grow deeper?
It means simply letting yourself
be filled with what is simple.

Letting yourself be filled
with simply-sitting-here,
until it fills you up,
until it completely
fulfils
you.

# EARTH-GRATITUDE

Letting myself notice
how I sit here on this ground
in my relationship to the earth,
how I can leave myself here,
release myself
down towards this earth.

That it carries me,
this earth,
and holds me!
That it has received me!
That it lets me breathe,
lets me grow,
lets me die,
lets me be!
Lets me!

Full of gratitude,
my breathing celebrates earth.

# EVENING QUESTION

Every evening I ask myself:
Have I lived today?
Am I really alive,
am I living now?

How can I know?
When I ask like this,
I actually do not know
what that could be,
really-living.

And if I
only stood there
or sat or lay down?
Would that be real life?
Simply standing there?
Sitting there?
Lying down?
Simply?

# NOT YET

Every night I know exactly:
Not yet!

I have not yet lived as
my own experience
keeps teaching me.

The old habit,
the centuries-old habit
of seeing things
as if they existed separately,

the habit
of regarding myself
as if there were an I,

this age old habit
which wants to deny
all experience of oneness,
no – I do not curse it!

By my seeing through it,
does not this habit
help me
to respect
the never ending 'not-yet'
as a way of eternal oneness?

## SUMMER EVENING

The light out there,
the space!
It makes sitting in silence
here inside
rather hard.

But why not let
all the light
and the wide space
enter here,
into my own silence?

Oh this light,
oh this space!

## NOW IS NOT

How would it be
if we could not tell the difference
between morning and evening?
And did not compare
this with that?

We would stumble
from one chaos into the next.

But what happens
when we cannot stop
distinguishing and comparing
for a single moment?

Moment after moment
we stumble
past the now.
For there is no comparison
in the experience of now.

Now is not wide and not narrow.
Now is not inside and not outside.
Now is not even silent.
Now is not even now.
Now is not
and is not not.

Is it not wonderful?
Now!

## HOW CAN IT GROW SILENT?

Sometimes,
just when silence wants to enter us
in the evening,
we feel acutely
that all that is not right with us
is still not right.

In the blink of an eye
we judge,
and cling to the judgement,
that we have not done better
and are not better,
and that this and that
has not yet
been put in order.

How can it grow silent
as long as not all is in order?
Perhaps we can inwardly
climb down a few steps,
down from the throne of entitlement,
in order to release ourselves into the evening's calm,
just as we are,
together with what is not right.
Perhaps we then find
that the silence envelops us
just as we are,
as if it were bringing together
what is breaking apart
through constant dividing
and obsessive judging.

## NOT A GOOD DAY

Today was not a good day.
It was a bad day,
a bad day.

Setting aside
hard blows of fate,
from where do we actually get
the criteria
for judging this day?

Well, would it be better
to be hypocritical with ourselves:
it was not really that bad!?

Perhaps, just for today,
we could also
simply take in
the whole effect of the day
without comment;

bring close to us,
bring into us
the whole effect of the day,
as if this today
simply and really
were part of ourselves,
really completely and just as it is,
part of ourselves.

Today was
what was.

## A GOOD DAY

What a good day!
The light-filled images
still spin
joyously
through my animated spirit.

What use is silence to me?
Today – really –
today I do not need it.

But at some point it enters anyway
and, almost unwelcome,
tones down the enthusiasm
but gradually I feel:
what a good day!
A day like every day!

# INDEPENDENCE

Sometimes fate brings us
unexpectedly into great distress
in which we come to feel acutely
how we depend on others.

And yet we sense in our innermost being
that in a fundamental way we are
completely independent.
So why do we fall into
such distress?

We forget that our own
deeply independent nature
is at the same time and always
completely bound up with
what we experience as dependent.

Independence itself seems to be
voluntarily, inseparably
bound up with being conditioned.

Just as we experience
the unconditioned silence
to be bound up
from moment to moment
with this breath we draw,
however it happens to be conditioned.

## LEAVING IT

In the evening –
perhaps –
with all our looking back
on the day which has passed,
we tend to withdraw from now-ness.

Suddenly, we have lost ourselves
in thinking about
what was, how it was,
and in thinking about
how it should have been different,

until with all our thinking
we cover over more and more
what was, how it was.

In our mind's eye, we could also
just place in front of us
what was,
simply place it in front of us,
in order to leave it
as it was,

so that we
ourselves,
together with what was,
connect again
with now-ness.

# MEGALOMANIA

Sitting in silence
is a practice
for the cure of megalomania.

The practice is
simply to let go,
breath by breath,
of the ego-image
with which we have to
elevate ourselves
in order to believe in our strength.

We can then experience
that the intrinsic strength living in us
is infinitely greater
than the most powerful delusion
we can construct for ourselves.

The practice is
simply to let go
of any image of ourselves whatever.

The healing intrinsic strength
will appear of its own accord.

## ATTACHED

Now that I am no longer
attached to it,
now all of a sudden
I receive everything
I was attached to.

Only what
I am attached to now,
I cannot
receive that.

# MOULDING

We are moulded.
Every one of us
is moulded
in our own incomparable way.

From top to bottom,
from outside to inside,
we are moulded –
by good experiences
which have promoted courage and trust,
also by disappointments
and excessive demands
which have caused
doubts and fears
and which are still slowing us down.

How might we be – not moulded?
We would not exist.

As soon as life
manifests itself as a living being,
it will be moulded
by thousands of conditions
which affect its growth.

As soon as life,
ungraspable and beyond differentiation,
manifests itself as a living being,
it takes on form
and with it differentiation.

It does not shrink from being moulded,
whether for good or ill.
It clearly trusts itself,
its living self.
It clearly believes
that in the final analysis,
through and beyond all the moulding,
IT itself, the ungraspable,
will be experienced and recognised.

Therefore, however valuable it is
for the sake of a good life
to work on our moulding,
that means, changing impediments
into something supportive,
what is still most important
is to look beyond
the moulding,
until we see
IT, life itself.

So I look at breath,
as it shapes itself
in my out and in which have been moulded
in this or that way.

So I look at silence,
which listens to itself
in the noises I make which have been moulded
in this or that way.

So I look at my thus
and see
the without-thus.

## DECEPTIVE THOUGHTS

If only these deceptive thoughts
and feelings did not
constantly come between,
between the silence and me.

I cannot keep up
with all the leaving be
and with all the letting go
of thousands and thousands of illusions.

How would it be then
if today, just for once,
I let go
of only one single deceptive thought,
only the one:
the thought that
something should
just now be different
from the way
it is?

Oh this silence –
this silence
between the silence
and me.

# TIGER, GOOSE, MOUSE AND MONKEY

If I gave a form
to the emotions
which sometimes emerge
as if they came out of the silence,

at one time a greedy tiger might sit
next to me, at another time a stupid goose.
Or it might be a helpless, anxious mouse,
then a crazy monkey,
or whatever we project
of human animality
onto innocent beasts.

I let the shadow animal,
or the whole crowd of them,
sit at my side.

I know they are part of me.
I invite them
to join
in my silence.

Strange, how their company
strengthens my composure.

And sometimes I experience
how they change
into courage or artlessness,
into respect and compassion.

# FEAR

Who would have expected it?
Some people are confronted with fear
precisely in the gentle light of sitting in silence.

With a fear which cannot be attached to anything,
to nothing at all.
That is exactly it.
This fear which is attached to nothing,
to a nothing.
Is it a nothing which rings out
so threateningly in the silence
when we seek what really is?

But for our ordinary consciousness,
what really is, is in fact
like nothing.
Because what really is
cannot be identified with anything,
not with beauty or clarity or light,
no, with nothing at all.
That is how it is with what really is.

So that, when we, with all our fear,
but trusting,
bring our silence
to this sound of nothing,
it turns out to be
the ungraspable
which confers meaning and plenitude
onto every something.
Onto every something,
like this one breath.

# THE QUIETER

The quieter we become,
the more we arrive
in the un-graspable,
at the threshold of which
we often react with fear,
even while we are drawn
to this home.

The quieter we become,
the more we arrive
in the forever-being
which expresses itself in
what arises
at this very moment
breathing in –
and fades away
breathing out.

# SILENCE MAKES US HAPPY

It is said
that silence makes us happy.

Should we,
can we, practise
being happy?

We can,
when we sit here in silence;
we could be on the lookout
within ourselves to see
whether anyone who is happy
can be found there.

However
we may feel just now,
we could look for
this happy one,
who, however we may feel just now,
is fundamentally and
imperturbably happy,
always.

# RECONCILIATION

Sometimes it is good
to direct the attention
to the moment of this very breath,
to this in,
to this out.

Sometimes it is good
to direct the attention
to the limitless expanse,
to the breathing horizon,
without paying heed to the difference
between 'in' and 'out'.

However we do it,
in the end the practice will lead
to the now; into this space
in which there is no opposition
between timeless expanse
and the clear contours of the moment.

In the end, the practice will lead
to the now; into this space
in which light and dark
do not contradict each other.

Therefore the experience of now
brings reconciliation
with all that was, how it was,
and opens up for all that will be
and leaves what is
as it just now is.

## THERE YOU SIT

There you sit in silence,
expecting the silence
which, for its part,
waits
in yourself
for yourself.

## PLAY

Sometimes sitting in silence
is like playing.

Full of thoughts
about the day gone by,
I play
sitting still.

I play it with my whole mind
so that I enter into
what I am playing.

I am aware of the friction
between my playing silence
and the un-silence in me.

And since I know
I am playing,
the play takes effect
until, right through the friction,
I become
more and more part
of what I play.

Until I become
what I play.
Until I become
silence.

# LOOKING

Sitting in silence we withdraw
from everyday occupations,
from movement and conversation.

If possible
we withdraw
from thoughts and feelings.

But sometimes, although we make an effort
and then let go again,
sometimes our feelings and thoughts
remain unconcerned.
They simply stay,
full of enthusiasm it seems,
they simply stay in place of silence.

What is to be done, if we are not to lose our own
enthusiasm?
I watch how they come,
thought images, feelings.
I see them come,
I see them being there.
I carry on looking.

Generally they move on
after a short time.
And even as I breathe with relief,
new ones wait in the wings.
I see them come, I see them being there,
I see them go, go and come.

I carry on looking.
At some point – I see looking.

## IN THE MIDST OF IT

After a short while,
when we have become silent,
all at once we are
in the midst of it,
in the midst of the silence.

In the experience of
in the midst of it
there is neither beginning nor end.
In the midst of it
there is only being.

Why not simply
let ourselves be in the midst of it,
without beginning,
without end,
in this silence,
in this breathing,
in this being?
In the midst of it.

# WINTER

In the middle of winter
opposites die
in a single
snow white.

In the middle of silence
merit and guilt,
good and evil
collapse
in a single light.

When shall we enter
into this experience?
Perhaps tonight,
perhaps in a dream.

## WINTER SOLSTICE

Cold time,
dark time,
inner time,
approaching the winter solstice.

And my own cold time,
dark time,
my own inner time –
do I allow it?

So that it too
makes its way towards a solstice?
So that it too,
like nature,
turns towards the light?

Just as breathing out
right now
turns to
breathing in.

Breath after breath,
after all the dark out-breath
in-breath comes
to me as light.

Breath after breath,
inner time,
winter solstice.

# I WONDER

It is rather strange
how this winter solstice
always comes back
just naturally,
whether we are concerned about it or not,
whether we think ourselves ready for it or not.

It always surprises me, too,
how these winter nights shine
and how they keep me awake
through my sleep.

I also find it amazing how –
despite all the suffering the world over –
so much that is wonderful,
small things that are wonderful
happen again and again
at this time.

As soon as I name what I mean,
it is not quite right.
If I were to say
I mean
how someone turns their head
to the window,
that is not quite right.

If I were to say
I mean
the sound
of a door falling shut,
that again is not quite right.

And yet these are the things
I mean.
They make me wonder
and wondering
makes me silent.

Just now I wonder
at how silent it is.

But that is not quite right either.
I wonder.

## ADVENT

Once again we can allow
ourselves to arrive
in this room,
at this place of ours.

Allow ourselves to breathe.
Let our mind and our senses
enter
the darkness of silence.

As if the gentle night
flowed around us
and protected us
from the thousand thoughts
which only a moment ago
filled our daytime consciousness.

As if a gentle darkness
enclosed us
and gathered us up
into being silent.

As if shining silence
waited in ourselves
as the I-myself.

## GOOD WILL

Does it not feel good
to sense our connection
with the ground again and again?
As if the earth
wished us well.

Does it not feel good
to sense the vast expanse above us?
As if the space of the heavens
wished us well.

Does it not feel endlessly good
to allow ourselves to be found
by silence again?
As if silence
wished us endlessly well.

Engaging with silence
we experience good will,
through and through,
wholly and completely.

Coming out from silence
we might wonder
at some point
how good will seems to seek
the way to the other
quite of its own accord,
through our very selves.

Therefore, whether we know it or not,
we never sit
only for our own good.

# SHARED SPACE

When we sit together
in silence,
of course each of us practises
in our own way.

Nevertheless, there is
this shared space
which creates a special strength
and concentration.

Is it possible to perceive
and acknowledge
how the practice of the others
supports us?

How do they do this?
It is best if they do nothing.
They just sit there in their silence.
This is what they do for me.

Just as I,
by sitting here in my silence,
am here for them.

Strange that we do not
recognise, always and everywhere,
how every presence
supports the presence
of each of us!
That we do not always recognise
the shared space.

## UNTIL

We practise until
practice leads us to a place
where there is no difference
between
the goal of our practice
and the practice itself.

Then practising is not practice.
Then there is only sitting here
and breathing
in freedom
and limitless gratitude.

Then
or now,
in this
moment.

# GUIDANCE ON PRACTICE

## ON POSTURE

An upright, well-balanced posture is conducive to sitting in silence. A straight backbone allows your breath to flow freely and helps to focus your mind.

Whatever sitting position you adopt, your knees should be lower than your pelvis because if your knees rise above the upper pelvic rim, either your back is automatically crooked or it tenses up in order to keep an upright posture.

Your shoulders are relaxed and your head is tall, as if the crown of your head were being pulled slightly upwards by a fine thread, leaving your chin somewhat tucked in.

If you sit on a chair, it should be as firm as possible. The sitting surface should not tilt forwards or backwards. In order to keep your knees lower than your pelvis you may have to put a blanket or cushion onto the chair. It is best to put your feet at a natural distance apart and parallel to each other, with their soles completely flat on the ground.

If you sit on the ground on a cushion or on a rolled-up blanket, you cross your legs so that either one foot is in front of the other, or one foot is placed on the calf or thigh of the other leg. If you can do so easily, you can cross your legs so far that each foot rests on the thigh of the other leg and the soles of your feet face upwards (lotus position).

Another possibility is to sit on your heels. In this position you can put a cushion or a blanket between your heels and your bottom to relieve the strain. Or you can sit on a low stool and put your feet pointing backwards between the sides of the stool, so that your toes face each other. This way your feet are not turned outwards, which could harm your hip joints.

For concentration it is helpful to lay your hands cupped inside each other (the left hand inside the right one) with the tips of your thumbs touching, so that an oval appears between your thumbs and first fingers. Your hands rest in contact with your body, with their sides one to two hand widths below your navel. Your arms form a rough circle so that your elbows do not touch your body.

It is best to keep your eyes slightly open so that you neither fix your gaze on a particular spot nor shut out the light in the room.

The same guidance on posture can be found in 'Living Silence' by Silvia Ostertag, Matador 2013.

# PICTURING THE FLOW OF BREATH

Letting yourself arrive in contact with the ground
and in connection with the space above your head.
Finding a good balance between a gentle pressure
on the ground
and a slight pull upwards.

Allowing your attention to gather
in the space above your head.
Guiding your attention like a flowing movement
through your whole body;
that is, through the space of your head,
through the space of your neck,
through the space of your chest and shoulders,
through the space of your waist,
through the space of your abdomen
and also through your legs
down into the earth.

Allowing your attention to rise again
round the outside in a broad arc,
to the right and left of your body,
perhaps also behind and in front of your body,
allowing it to rise again to the space above your head,
from where it now flows down again
through your whole body into the earth.

When you have imagined this movement
and inwardly enacted it several times,
the flow of your breath will tend to link with it of its own
accord.

It is best when the inner downward flowing movement
joins with the out-breath,
and the outer rising movement
accompanies the in-breath.

So that the out-breath flows through your whole body,
as if from the space above your head
down into the earth,
to change there to in-breath
and as such to rise again round the outside.

After a while it may be
that in breathing out, the inner flowing movement
right through the body awakens an opposing energy
which at the same time tends upwards.
If it appears of its own accord,
this flowing counter tension
will naturally support
your upright posture.

In general the image of your breath may expand,
or become more detailed, or change.
But as simple a form as possible is the most favourable
for entering into silence.
For the only point
of this guided attention
is to be able to participate inwardly
in the process of your breathing.

The inspiration for this guidance came from working with Karl
Metzler, mime and body work teacher, St. Ulrich near Freiburg. It
can also be found in 'Living Silence' by Silvia Ostertag, Matador
2013.

The Oxford Zen Centre was founded by Sister Elaine Macinnes in 1993, in the tradition of Sanbo-Zen, part of the world-wide Zen community, which has its origin in Kamakura, Japan. In the UK, weekly meetings are held in Oxford and in London and longer retreats are also offered in the UK and abroad.

For further information and additional copies of this book, please contact the Centre through its website at: www.oxfordzencentre.org.uk

'Finding Silence' is also available as an e-book.

'Living Silence', Silvia Ostertag's first book, published by Matador in English in 2013, can also be obtained both from the Oxford Zen Centre and as an e-book.

Susanne Ehrhardt and Wendy Tyndale, the translators of these two books, are writers and practitioners in the tradition of Sanbo-Zen.